WHAT HAPPENED HERE?

TUDOR WARSHIP

Elizabeth Newbery
Photographs by Richard Hubbard
Illustrations by Gillian Clements

Contents

A & C BLACK · LONDON

The Mary Rose

This book is about a warship called the *Mary Rose*. King Henry VIII ordered the ship to be built about 500 years ago in Tudor times. She was named after Mary, Henry's younger sister, and the rose which was a badge of Tudor kings and queens.

The *Mary Rose* was the pride of Henry's navy, and for 34 years the ship fought in battles against the French. But on 19th July 1545, she capsized and sank just off the coast at Portsmouth. There were over 400 men on board. Fewer than 35 were saved.

For nearly 450 years, the *Mary Rose* lay under 12-14 metres of water partly protected by deep mud. In 1982 archaeologists recovered the ship from the seabed. The objects found on board were brought up first. Then the remains of the hull were raised. Scientists, called conservators, cleaned, restored and dried the hull and the objects, so that archaeologists could study them.

The children in this book wanted to know what archaeologists had found out about the *Mary Rose*. They wanted to discover more about life at sea in Tudor times. The children began their investigation in Portsmouth, Hampshire, where the remains of the *Mary Rose* can be seen. In the photographs some of the children are wearing copies of the jerkins that were found on board the ship.

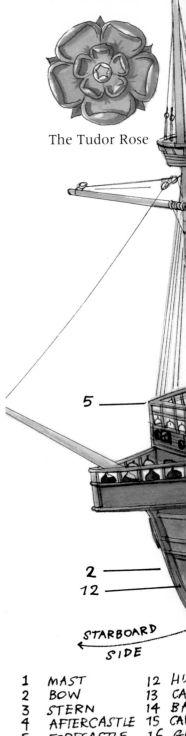

The Tudor Rose

STARBOARD
SIDE

1	MAST	12	H'
2	BOW	13	CA
3	STERN	14	B
4	AFTERCASTLE	15	CA
5	FORECASTLE	16	G
6	CASTLE DECK	17	G
7	UPPER DECK	18	K
8	MAIN DECK	19	Y
9	ORLOP DECK		
10	HOLD		
11	SHIP'S GALLEY & OVEN		

C.942.05

0892533577

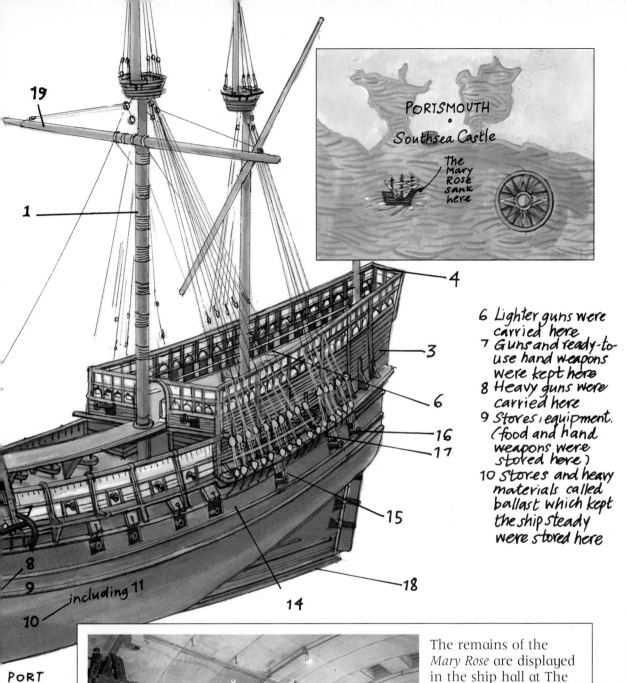

19

1

PORTSMOUTH
•
Southsea Castle

The
Mary
Rose
sank
here

4

3

6

16

17

15

6 Lighter guns were
carried here
7 Guns and ready-to-
use hand weapons
were kept here
8 Heavy guns were
carried here
9 Stores, equipment.
(food and hand
weapons were
stored here)
10 Stores and heavy
materials called
ballast which kept
the ship steady
were stored here

8

9

including 11

10

18

14

PORT
SIDE

The remains of the
Mary Rose are displayed
in the ship hall at The
Mary Rose Exhibition
in Portsmouth. There,
the children saw the
hull being sprayed with
chemicals to preserve
it. The children could
see inside the remaining
half of the ship, with
three of her four decks
in position.

3

How do we know about the Mary Rose?

When the *Mary Rose* sank, life on board stopped. The ship is like a time capsule which gives a picture of just one particular day – 19th July 1545.

Objects

The largest object recovered was the hull. By studying it, archaeologists learned a lot about the way Tudor ships were built. Smaller objects found on board, such as clothing and weapons, tell us about life at sea and on land in Tudor times.

The silts

The fine silt, or mud, which filled the hull soon after the *Mary Rose* sank have preserved a lot of very important evidence. Seeds, fruit stones, meat and fish bones show what the crew ate. The children thought that the remains of insects and the bones of a young rat found in the silt might be evidence about the health of the crew and their living conditions.

When the *Mary Rose* sank, she lay on her side. The port side was open to currents in the water and small creatures which gradually bored their way into the timbers. But the starboard side was buried in mud. Over time all the uppermost timbers were destroyed, leaving only the buried part behind. The picture shows the remains of the hull being raised in 1982.

◄

This diver is using a suction machine called an airlift to remove silt from around the remains of the *Mary Rose*.

This boy looked at an exhibit which shows how layers of silt built up round the *Mary Rose* over hundreds of years. There are many objects in the silt. Those which are buried deepest and nearest to the hull are the oldest. Those found in the top layer of silt are more modern. The boy is holding a gun flint (used to set a gun off) which is about 200 years old. The clay pipe is about a hundred years old.

Documents

Archaeologists have used other kinds of evidence to learn more about the *Mary Rose*. Documents such as bills, letters and lists of goods also give us information about why the ship was built and what was on board. One of the most interesting documents is the Anthony Roll. This lists all the men, weapons and ammunition on the *Mary Rose*, so it was possible to check off the weapons as they were brought up and work out which items are still missing.

Oily, soft, firm mud

Slipper limpets 1900–1920

clay pipe

gun flint

Collapsed Timber

This picture of the *Mary Rose* comes from the Anthony Roll (a list of all the King's ships). It was painted in 1546, a year after she sank.

Time-lines

The first time-line shows some of the important events which took place during Henry VIII's reign. The second time-line shows some of the important events in the history of the *Mary Rose*, up to the present day.

Henry VIII's reign

1509

1509-1547 Henry VIII is king. He inherits five warships from his father, Henry VII. The Kings of France and Spain, and the Pope (head of the Roman Catholic faith), are the most powerful rulers in Europe. There are three wars with France during Henry's reign. Ship building is an important industry right through the Tudor period. Many new warships are built, including the *Mary Rose*. Merchant ships are also hired to fight in the wars.

1510-1520 Henry VIII invites foreign craftsmen to make guns in London.

1516-1521 A Portuguese captain, Ferdinand Magellan, becomes the first person to sail right round the world.

Main events on the Mary Rose

1509

1509 Henry VIII orders the *Mary Rose* to be built in Portsmouth. She costs about £350 to build, a huge sum of money in those days, and is one of the largest ships in the fleet.

1511 The *Mary Rose* is finished. She is taken up the Thames and loaded with guns, bows and arrows and ammunition from the Tower of London. She fights in three French wars and helps to capture over 30 French ships.

1536 *Mary Rose* is rebuilt and upgraded to 700 tonnes. She is fitted with new cannons.

1545 The *Mary Rose* capsizes and sinks 2 km (1.25 miles) out from the entrance to Portsmouth harbour. The loss of an important ship was (and still is) a major disaster. Expert salvage men are brought in from Venice to try to raise her but they are unsuccessful.

1534 Henry VIII declares himself head of the Church of England. Roman Catholic monasteries are closed by force. Henry takes their lands and riches, and keeps them for himself and his friends.

Henry wants more power for himself. He sides first with Spain against France, and then with France against Spain.

1538-1544 Henry VIII builds and strengthens castles and small forts along the south coast to protect England against invasions. Southsea Castle near Portsmouth is built in 1544. The fortifications which protect Portsmouth are strengthened. By the end of his life Henry has formed a navy with nearly 60 warships.

1547 Henry VIII dies.

1836 Victorian divers, John and Charles Deane, discover the wreck. They lift and sell off objects. Then the wreck is forgotten again.

1965-1979 Divers re-discover the Mary Rose. The ship is surveyed using scientific equipment.

1979-82 The ship is uncovered. The objects are surveyed, photographed and lifted. Over 19,000 objects are raised. The silts are excavated. The structure of the ship is surveyed and photographed. Preparations begin to raise the remains of the hull from the sea-bed.

11 October 1982 The remains of hull are raised and placed in a dry dock, now called the ship hall. This is very close to where archaeologists think the *Mary Rose* was built in Tudor times. Conservators begin work on preserving the timbers. Archaeologists examine the objects brought up and study the hull.

How was the Mary Rose built?

The children learned that Tudor ships were made mostly of oak. This is because oak is a very strong wood which does not rot easily and is quite easy to shape with hand tools. The shipwright in charge of making the *Mary Rose* selected the best oaks from forests in the South of England. He looked for tall, good-quality trees. These provided wood for the long, straight planks needed to build the decks. He also looked for trees with good, strong branches growing at right angles to the trunk. They provided naturally curved wood needed for making other parts of the ship.

After cutting down the trees, the trunks were trimmed of any unwanted side branches and divided up. Some trunks were 'cleft' or split down their length to make planks for the 'castles' at each end of the ship. This produced planks which were less likely to shrink or split than sawn planks.

These boys tried cleaving planks by hammering in wooden wedges to split the timber down the length of its trunk. They discovered that the secret was knowing where to put the wedges. One boy hit the wedge with a hammer called a maul. The other boy checked to see that the wood was splitting straight. The tree was split into halves, quarters, eighths and so on to make thinner and thinner planks.

The huge curved timbers needed to strengthen the joints between the hull and the deck were hewn, or cut from the curved parts of the tree. They were roughly shaped with an axe and finished with an adze. The timbers were mostly held together with oak pegs, although iron bolts and iron nails were also used. The pegs, bolts and nails were all made by hand.

▲

The children watched a shipwright finish a curved timber with an adze. They were surprised that he could give the timber such a smooth surface using such a simple tool.

Some wood was probably sawn on trestles, similar to those shown here. The children realised that sawing by hand was much harder work than sawing with modern power tools.

▼

Elm, which lasts a long time in salt water, was used to make the keel (the spine of the ship which runs along the bottom). Some woods such as elm could not be cleft easily and had to be cut up using hand saws similar to those used today. Poorer quality woods, such as poplar and pine which soak up water and become soft when wet, were used inside the ship.

9

Setting sail

In Tudor times a ship pilot had only simple equipment and the stars to guide him across oceans. He used a magnetic compass to steer in the right direction. He measured the depth of the sea and tested the sea-bed with a sounding lead. The lead had a shallow hollow in its base filled with sticky tallow, or animal fat. Mud, sand or pebbles stuck to this showing the pilot what the sea-bed under the ship was like. This helped him work out where the ship was. He used features ashore such as headlands, beaches, lighthouses and castles to pinpoint the position of the ship.

Tudor sailors also worked out where the ship was using charts, tide tables and pilots' books. These contained details of the coastline, sea-bed, winds, the depth of the water, and the whereabouts of dangerous tides and reefs. However, no tide tables or pilots' books have been discovered on board the *Mary Rose* so far.

The heavy canvas sails were hung from stout yard-arms. These had to be hoisted up with ropes to make the sails fill with wind. The parrel ribs and parrel balls acted like giant ball-bearings. They allowed the heavy yard-arm to slide up and down the mast.

This girl is lowering a sounding lead to measure the depth of the water beneath the ship.

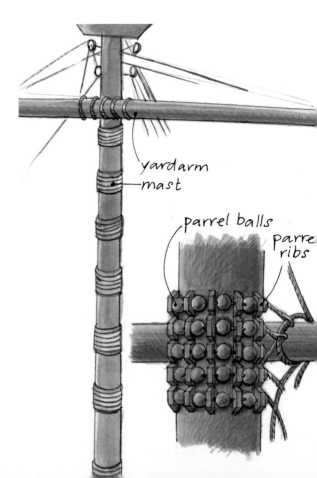

yardarm

mast

parrel balls

parre ribs

▲ These parrels were found still stored in a neat bundle on the orlop deck of the wreck.

▲ The children raised a yard-arm up a model of a mast using a copy of the equipment found on the *Mary Rose*. Using ropes and pulley blocks they all pulled together. They expected it to be hard work but were amazed how efficient the equipment was, and how easily they moved the heavy weight.

The children learned how Tudor sailors worked out how fast the ship was travelling. The sailors threw a rope overboard. One end was attached to a wooden reel. The other end was attached to a thin chip of wedge-shaped wood which kept the rope afloat in the water. The rope was tied with equally-spaced knots. As the ship moved forward, the line unravelled from the reel and the knots were counted over a known distance. We still use the word 'knot' to describe speed at sea.

A Tudor sailor measuring the speed of the ship by counting the knots on the rope attached to the floating chip.

A day at sea

The crew of the *Mary Rose* was divided into two 'shifts' called the port and starboard watches. Each man had a partner on the opposite watch. They shared a sleeping space and, while one man was "off watch" sleeping, the other was "on watch" helping to work the ship, maintaining vital equipment, making repairs and setting the sails.

The pattern of the day aboard a ship in Tudor times was ruled by a strict timetable, rather like a modern school day. The children learned that there were no clocks on board. On a ship, time was measured with a sandglass. This was like a giant egg timer. A measured amount of sand trickled from one part into the other in exactly half an hour. When the glass was turned to start again, the ship's bell was rung. The children thought that the ship's bell must have been as important for keeping time as a school bell is today.

Sundials were also used to tell the time. Nine have been found on board the *Mary Rose*. Sundials worked during the day when the sun was out, but not when it was cloudy or at night.

While not on watch or sleeping, sailors passed the time making music, or playing games such as dice, backgammon and nine men's morris (a game with rules similar to noughts and crosses). Sometimes the men fished over the side of the ship.

Gambling and board games were popular in Tudor times. This backgammon set was made of oak and decorated with different coloured woods inlaid into the board. It was found in the cabin belonging to the ship's carpenter.

◄

The girl is examining a sandglass. The boy is examining the words on the ship's bell brought up from the *Mary Rose*. The words are "I was made in the year 1510". As the *Mary Rose* was built between 1509 and 1511, the children thought that the bell might have been made especially for her.

These pipes and the remains of a fiddle, or violin, were found aboard the *Mary Rose*. Music was used on board ships for entertainment, and may have helped everyone to keep rhythm when pulling on the ropes.

13

Shipmates

There were two groups of men aboard the *Mary Rose* – soldiers and sailors. Soldiers were responsible for fighting. They were either hired or forced to join the navy and fight for the King. Henry VIII also hired foreign mercenaries. Mercenaries were soldiers who fought for anyone who would pay them. Sailors were responsible for   sailing the ship. The soldiers and sailors had their own officers, but everyone was under the command of the Captain.

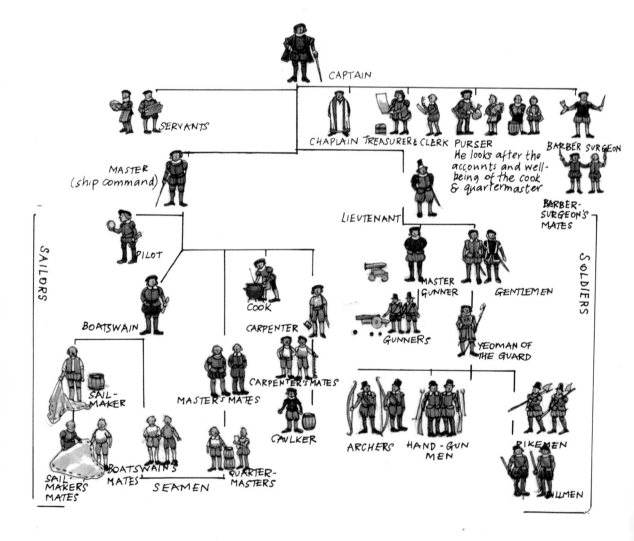

Who was who aboard a Tudor warship in about 1540.

The children found evidence to show that the Captain and the officers of the *Mary Rose* were well educated. Archaeologists have found books, writing equipment such as an ink pot, quills, seals and even bits of pages with writing on them. They have also discovered several wooden chests which contained personal possessions. One contained a piece of carved ivory which probably came from a decorative box made in Italy. The children decided that the person who owned the chest must have been quite wealthy, perhaps one of the officers.

Some of the objects inside an oak chest found on the *Mary Rose*.

We know that some of the soldiers and sailors aboard the *Mary Rose* could not read or write. Many of their possessions have simple marks cut into them so that the men could recognise them quickly and easily.

Some of the men on board the *Mary Rose* kept their working equipment and personal possessions in wooden chests. This chest was found on the main deck at the stern of the ship.

A purse found in a chest on the *Mary Rose* may have contained gold coins called Angels, a Half Angel and a Crown of the Double Rose. An Angel was about two months' pay for a member of the crew.

Going to war!

The hulls of ships built before Tudor times were constructed from overlapping planks. Their gun-ports could not be made waterproof, so these ship carried guns only on their upper decks. But too many guns made these ships top-heavy and likely to capsize.

The hull of the *Mary Rose* was made of planks which butted together. Her gun-port lids fitted tightly into the hull, and when closed they were watertight. So the *Mary Rose* could carry extra guns on her lower decks, close to the waterline.

The children found that the *Mary Rose* had two main types of gun. There were 15 heavy bronze guns which were loaded from the front. This is called muzzle-loading. These guns were fitted on to carriages with wheels, so that they could be pulled back inside the ship to be cleaned out and re-loaded.

▲

These boys lifted a model of a breech chamber for an iron gun. They learned that first the gun was loaded with a large ball of stone, called shot. Then the breech chamber containing the gunpowder was slotted into the back of the gun.

This boy pretended to load gunpowder with a powder scoop into the barrel of a bronze muzzle-loading gun. The girl pretended to wait at the ready with a rammer to push the gunpowder well down into the barrel.

▼

A cross section of a breech-loading iron gun. Breech-loading guns were deadliest when fired at close range.

There were 54 lighter iron guns which were loaded from behind. This is called breech-loading. Gunpowder was loaded into removable compartments called breech chambers, which slotted into the back of the guns. Spare breech chambers were kept handy so that the guns could be re-loaded and fired rapidly. The soldiers also carried handguns, pikes, bills, swords and daggers for hand-to-hand fighting, in case the enemy managed to get aboard.

A linstock held a piece of smouldering rope called a match. The gunner held the linstock at arm's length and lit the gunpowder with it. ▶

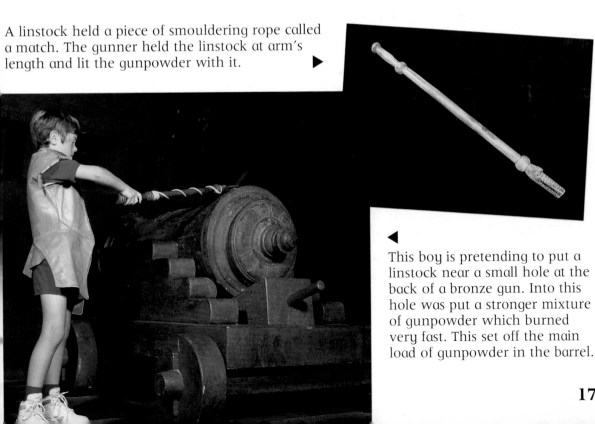

◀ This boy is pretending to put a linstock near a small hole at the back of a bronze gun. Into this hole was put a stronger mixture of gunpowder which burned very fast. This set off the main load of gunpowder in the barrel.

Gunpowder and shot

Almost anything can be fired from a gun! In Tudor times, shot, the ammunition for guns, was usually made from stone, iron or lead. Some iron shot found aboard the *Mary Rose* had large iron spikes going through them. The spikes may have been designed to stick into the side of an enemy ship and, if so, the shot was probably coated with a special material which would burn.

Smaller guns fired small cubes of iron, flakes of flint or pebbles. These were either placed loose in the barrel, or put in wooden canisters which were loaded into the guns. This ammunition was used against an enemy crew or aimed at mast and sails, or rigging. Shooting rigging was a good tactic against a wind-powered vessel because if it was damaged, the ship went out of control. Chemicals such as quicklime were also fired at the enemy. These burnt everything and everyone who came into contact with them.

These boys tried using simple wooden gauges to measure the size of the shot. If the shot was too large it would stick in the barrel and burst the gun. If it was too small, it would rattle around in the barrel when the gun was being fired and would not travel in a straight line.

Henry VIII's coat of arms on a bronze cannon. Henry VIII was very proud of his new and powerful warship, the *Mary Rose*.

But guns and gunpowder were dangerous to use. One stray spark could blow up a ship, so gunpowder was stored in barrels, away from the guns. The extra-strong powder needed to set off the main charges was kept in closed powder flasks. Cannons were kept securely fastened with ropes to stop them crashing around in a storm, and damaging the ship and crew.

These girls discovered that the ladder (or companionway) between the upper and main deck was very steep. They decided that shifting heavy stone shot for the iron guns on the upper deck would have been very difficult when the ship was rolling around.

19

Archers and longbows

In Tudor times, longbows and arrows were used for sport as well as for war. The children were astonished to learn that boys were given their first bows when they were about seven years old. They learned how to use them when they were very young, but they had still to practice continually until they were either too old or ill to be able to use them any longer.

The *Mary Rose* carried a force of professional archers and their equipment. The archers had to be very strong and fit, able to fire about 10-12 arrows a minute for hours on end without a break. The children discovered that archers on the upper decks of the *Mary Rose* were protected by moveable panels, or blinds, in front of them and a heavy net over their heads. This net stopped the enemy from boarding the ship, but it also prevented the men from escaping as the *Mary Rose* sank.

Archaeologists have recovered 137 complete bows and 3,500 arrows from the *Mary Rose*. Some bows were found still stored in boxes on the orlop deck. Others were found ready for use on the upper deck at the stern. Bows were made from the wood of yew trees which was very strong and pliable.

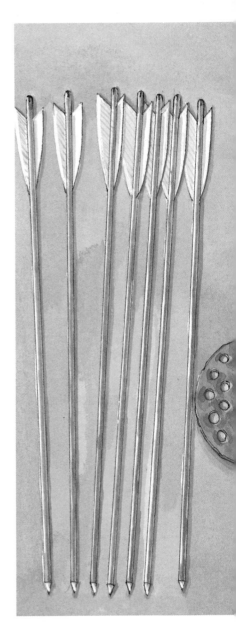

Arrows were usually about 80cm long, and made from poplar, beech, hazel and ash wood which grows straight so the arrows flew true. Flight feathers came from geese and swans.

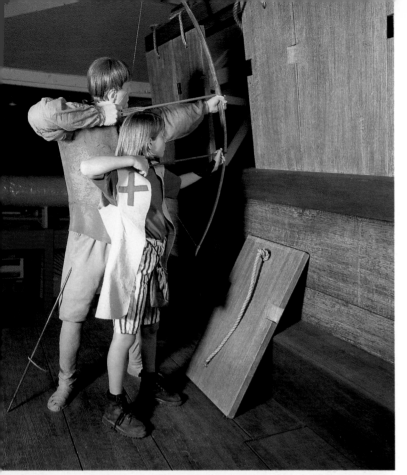

This boy moved a blind to see how it fitted into position. He found it could be lifted away to make a port hole for an archer. He also learned that it was made of poplar which is lighter than oak. But he still found it heavy to lift!

◄

This girl tried placing an arrow on a copy of a bow found aboard the *Mary Rose*. She needed all her strength to pull back the bowstring. The length of an archer's bow depended on how tall he was. Bows found on the *Mary Rose* range in length between 1.60 metres and 2.06 metres.

Archers wore wrist-guards to protect their arms from the bowstring as it sprang back. Those found aboard the *Mary Rose* were decorated with elaborate patterns.

▼

21

Keeping shipshape

The *Mary Rose* was often at sea for many months. In quiet times the men on board had to keep the ship and the equipment in tip-top condition. They patched sails with canvas, mended nets, caulked, or painted the decks with pitch to keep them watertight, they checked the rigging, and repaired any ropes that were frayed or split.

Every day the crew had to sweep the decks, and make sure that the water channels and drains were clear. If these became clogged and water was not able to escape, the ship's timbers would become damp and rot. The men also had to make sure that the guns were cleaned and in perfect working order.

This picture shows some of the items made by sailors on board the *Mary Rose*. They include a half-made shot, a shot-mould, a half-finished linstock, sewing equipment, and a knife sheath which was probably carved at sea.

The crew were responsible for keeping their own clothes and possessions in good repair. Ribbons, thread, buttons, pins and thimbles have been discovered on the wreck. Some items of clothing have been found neatly mended. One discovery was a knitted detachable sleeve or legging, called a scogger, which was worn to keep out the cold. However, no knitting needles have been found so far.

Archaeologists have discovered a bag of leather shoes and a sole cut out of the side of an old leather bucket. The children thought that this was good evidence that there might have a cobbler on board the ship.

This large grindstone was found on the orlop deck at the bow of the ship. It was used for sharpening knives, tools and weapons at sea.

The children tried weaving using a copy of a loom found aboard the *Mary Rose*. The loom produced a strap which the children thought might have been used to help lift things on board.

Preparing food on board

Before the *Mary Rose* was discovered, we knew very little about what was eaten on Tudor ships. We did know from documents that food supplies were delivered by smaller ships, called victuallers. There are many stories of ships running out of food, especially in bad weather or war, when supplies could not be delivered.

Archaeologists have uncovered the remains of food stored aboard the *Mary Rose*. We now know that the crew ate beef, pork, lamb, venison (deer) and fish – especially cod from the North Sea. The men also had fresh fruit and vegetables such as plums and damsons. Many foods were salted or smoked to stop them going bad, but some of the meat and fish was fresh. The children were surprised to learn that baskets full of newly gutted and trimmed cod ready to be cooked or stored were found on the *Mary Rose*.

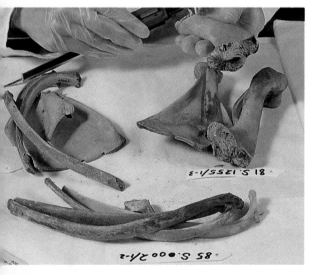

An archaeologist examines pig bones found in the silt. Meat was found cut up in individual portions and stored in barrels. Marrow bones and offal, such as liver and kidney, were not included because they went bad quickly and spoiled the rest of the meat.

All the food eaten on the *Mary Rose* was prepared by cooks in the ship's galley in the hold. Huge fish and meat stews for the crew were cooked in cauldrons. The officers may have had special meals cooked in small pots. There was a brick oven on board so bread may have been freshly baked. Archaeologists have also discovered the remains of leather water buckets near the galley. These were probably kept close by in case of fire.

The children saw an enormous copper cauldron in which food for the crew was cooked. They noticed it had a huge lip made of lead which held it in place. Two cauldrons were placed on top of a brick firebox which contained a log fire. A stack of logs has even been recovered from the wreck.

cauldron

brick firebox

This boy tried out a pair of bellows. He discovered that they pumped air. Bellows were used to make the fires burn more fiercely. The bricks come from the galley on the *Mary Rose*.

Eating and drinking

In Tudor times, everyone ate their food with a knife and a spoon. Forks were not used for eating in England until the mid-1600s. Knives were also used for other purposes such as cutting rope or carving. Very little pottery or glass has been found aboard the ship. The children wondered if this was because, being breakable, not much was used on board ship.

The officers, who usually came from wealthy families, ate from pewter plates. Pewter is a metal made from tin and lead. They drank wine and beer from pewter tankards. The soldiers and sailors ate from wooden plates. They drank beer from leather flaggons or wooden tankards lined with pitch or tar to make them watertight.

▲
Fine pewter recovered from the *Mary Rose*.

These wooden bowls and dish are part of a large collection of everyday items found on board the *Mary Rose*. When everyday things became damaged on land in Tudor times, people did not usually save them. So now these ordinary things are some of the most important objects recovered from the *Mary Rose*.

▼

These children tried drinking from copies of a leather flask and a wooden tankard. The boy is grinding peppercorns in a pepper mill.

The children learned that peppercorns were found aboard the *Mary Rose*. They were amused to discover that not only was pepper used to improve the flavour of food, it was also taken as a medicine by men suffering from wind.

The crew ate their meals at the end of their watches. They probably ate where they kept watch, or where they slept. No one knows for sure when or where the officers ate their food.

Keeping the crew healthy

The ship had to be manned at all times so keeping the crew fit and healthy was most important. Most ships carried a doctor and his mate. In Tudor times, the doctor was called a barber-surgeon. As a barber he shaved the men, trimmed their beards, cut their hair and got rid of their head lice. As a doctor he provided medicines and lotions, healed wounds and cut off limbs if they were badly injured or infected.

Archaeologists have discovered the chest belonging to the barber-surgeon on the *Mary Rose*. Inside it were some of his medicines and instruments. Nearby was a metal bleeding bowl, which was used to catch the blood in operations, a mortar for mixing medicines and a barber's bowl used to hold shaving water. The archaeologists even found bandages soaked in herbal lotions ready for use.

This chest belonged to the barber-surgeon. It contained his equipment, including spatulas for spreading ointment on to wounds, a syringe and a wooden feeding bottle for men too ill to eat, or for those with injuries to their faces. The children were amazed to learn that some wooden containers found in the chest were still filled with ointment.

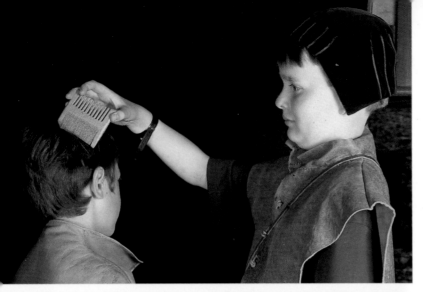

This boy is pretending to de-lice hair using a copy of a comb found on board the *Mary Rose*. The children noticed that it was very similar to the combs used to get rid of head lice today. The boy is wearing a copy of a velvet barber-surgeon's hat found on board.

The barber-surgeon's cabin was on the main deck. It had a very low ceiling and was very dark and cramped. The children decided there was hardly room to bandage a leg. They wondered how the barber-surgeon managed to amputate limbs in such a small space.

Life on board ship was crowded and cramped. There were no washrooms. No lavatories have been discovered so far although one chamber pot has been found. The children guessed that the ship probably stank. Archaeologists have uncovered a pomander – a small container filled with sweet-smelling herbs. An officer probably held it to his nose when the smells aboard the ship became too bad.

How to find out more

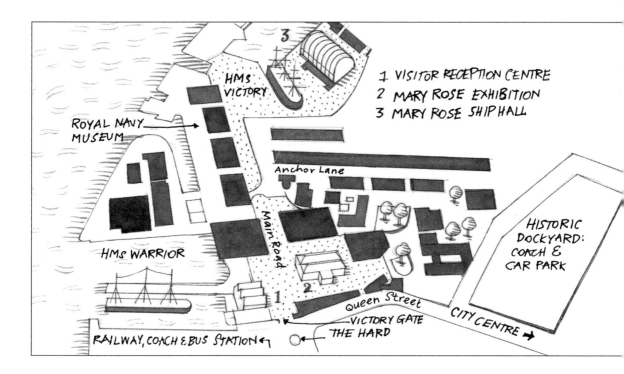

Labels on map:
HMS VICTORY
ROYAL NAVY MUSEUM
Anchor Lane
Main Road
HMS WARRIOR
1 VISITOR RECEPTION CENTRE
2 MARY ROSE EXHIBITION
3 MARY ROSE SHIP HALL
HISTORIC DOCKYARD: COACH & CAR PARK
Queen Street
VICTORY GATE
THE HARD
CITY CENTRE →
RAILWAY, COACH & BUS STATION ←

You can find out much more about life at sea in Tudor times by visiting The Mary Rose Ship Hall and Exhibition, HM Naval Base, Portsmouth PO1 3LX. Tel: 01705 839766.

Visits

Close by the *Mary Rose* Exhibition are the Royal Naval Museum, HMS Victory and HMS Warrior. Together they tell of life at sea from Tudor times up to the present day.

The Defences of Portsmouth
You can still see the defences around Portsmouth that Henry enlarged and made safer. The best place to explore is near the Square and Round towers, and connecting wall, in Old Portsmouth.

Portsmouth Cathedral
Archaeologists have uncovered many of the bones of the men who went down with the *Mary Rose*. They found that most of the young men were strong and healthy. One crew member has now been buried in a special grave in Portsmouth Cathedral.

Southsea Castle
Henry VIII ordered Southsea Castle, Southsea, Hampshire to be built, to help defend the south coast against invasions from Europe. It was from here that Henry watched in horror as the *Mary Rose* sank.

30

Things to do

Here are some ideas for things to do which could help you find out more about life at sea in Tudor times.

How to make a magnetic compass

You will need: a bar magnet; a darning needle; a saucer of water; a compass; a cork

First magnetise the darning needle. To do this lay the needle on a flat surface and stroke it end to end 30 times in the same direction with the same end of the bar magnet.

Balance the needle on the cork. Float the needle and the cork on a saucer of water. It should point north and south. Use the other compass to check its direction.

Make a sandglass

You will need: a clean dry plastic bottle with a cap; a clean dry glass jar; dry sand (silver sand not builders' sand) or salt; a fine sieve or a pair of old tights; a sharp knife, paper and rubber bands.

Make sure that the plastic bottle will rest upside-down in the neck of the jar. Sift the sand or salt through the sieve or tights to make sure there are no lumps.

Make a small hole in the bottle's cap (ask an adult to help you). Cut the base of the bottle. Fill the bottle with sand.

Fit the bottle upside-down into the neck of the glass jar. How long does it take for the bottle to empty completely?

Make a paper scale. Fix your scale to the outside of the jar with rubber bands. How long does it take for the sand to reach each mark on your scale?

Can you make a scale that will measure in minutes?

Index

First published 1996
A & C Black (Publishers) Limited
35 Bedford Row
London WC1R 4JH
ISBN 0-7136-4170-3

© 1996 A & C Black (Publishers) Limited

A CIP catalogue record for this book is available from the British Library

Acknowledgements

The author and publisher would like to thank the *Mary Rose* Trust: Andy Elkerton (Head of Documentation), Alex Hildred (Head of Research/Interpretation), Maggie Richards (Researcher), Mark Griffin (Visitor Services Manager), Dr Mark Jones (Head of Conservation), Sue Bickerton, Glen McConnachie (Conservation), Christopher Dobbs (Head of Research/Information), Charles Pochin, Peter Crossman, Colin McKewan (Interpreters), Roger Purkis (Illustration); Portsmouth Grammar School, Brian Sheldrick, James Monk, Nicholas Perry, Sarah Peters, Celine Reddy, Christopher Walker; Bay House School, Gosport, Wasseem El Sarraj

All photographs by Richard Hubbard (the *Mary Rose* Trust) and the *Mary Rose* Archive.

Photograph of the Anthony Roll by kind permission of the Master and Fellows, Magdalene College, Cambridge.
Layout of the diagram on page 14 by P. Whitlock (the *Mary Rose* Trust)

Typeset in Meriden Infant 14/17pt

Printed and bound in Italy by Partenaires Fabrication, Malesherbes, France.